PRAYING WITH
THE ENGLISH POETS

The PRAYING WITH series

PRAYING WITH SAINT AUGUSTINE
Introduction by Murray Watts

PRAYING WITH SAINT FRANCIS
Introduction by David Ford

PRAYING WITH HIGHLAND CHRISTIANS
Introduction by Sally Magnusson

PRAYING WITH THE NEW TESTAMENT
Introduction by Joyce Huggett

PRAYING WITH SAINT TERESA
Introduction by Elaine Storkey

PRAYING WITH THE JEWISH TRADITION
Introduction by Lionel Blue

PRAYING WITH THE OLD TESTAMENT
Introduction by Richard Holloway

PRAYING WITH THE ORTHODOX TRADITION
Preface by Kallistos Ware

PRAYING WITH THE ENGLISH HYMN WRITERS
Compiled and Introduced by Timothy Dudley-Smith

PRAYING WITH THE ENGLISH MYSTICS
Compiled and Introduced by Jenny Robertson

PRAYING WITH THE ENGLISH TRADITION
Compiled and Introduced by Margaret Pawley

Other titles in preparation

PRAYING WITH

The English Poets

Compiled and introduced by
RUTH ETCHELLS

TRiANGLE

First published 1990
Triangle
SPCK
Holy Trinity Church
Marylebone Road
London NW1 4DU

British Library Cataloguing in Publication Data
Praying with the English poets.
1. Christian life. Prayer – Devotional works
I. Etchells, Ruth
242.8
ISBN 0-281-04482-1

Typeset by Rowland Phototypesetting Ltd
Bury St Edmunds, Suffolk
Printed in Great Britain by
BPCC Hazell Books
Aylesbury, Bucks
Member of BPCC Ltd

CONTENTS

INTRODUCTION

Prayer is the disposition of the heart towards God. As such, it has both its listening and its outpouring: often woven together, or in antithesis. It is another word for the way, at all levels of our being, we live in relation to God, who creates us and keeps us safe and brings us home to him, matured in the grace of his Son's loving goodness to us. So the language of prayer is the language of this constant interchange between each of us and God, groups of us and God, the whole Christian family in space and time, and God. It ranges from the inarticulate moan and groaning to him of our periods of wretchedness from whatever reason, through the stumblings, or the articulacy, of the heart in lively dialogue with God in seasons of doubt, contentment, stimulus, flatness, thankfulness and questioning, to the ecstatic stillness that some blessed souls enjoy in a rapture of gazing upon their Lord. It includes the formal loveliness of the churches' liturgies, the silence of the Quaker meeting, and the jubilant outburst of those speaking 'in tongues' within charismatic communities. Above all it is interchange. So its language is both address to, and response to, God: listening and responding; addressing and listening: its vocabulary and grammar will include both elements of such dialogue.

It follows that poems which pray will also be listening or outpouring or both, and they will include the same ranges of mood, of hope and dereliction and exaltation and angst. Moreover, such poems will not always be in 'high' language, just as prayer itself is not always in 'high' language. Indeed, the mystery of prayer has this in common with the mystery of poetry, that their language ranges from the commonplace and the (literally) mundane, to fervency, exaltation, and rapt stillness. Noisy as gongs, quiet as breath, musical, abrasive, an undertone, a declamation, 'a kind of tune which all things hear and fear':

> Prayer the Church's banquet, Angel's age,
> God's breath in man returning to his birth,
> The soul in paraphrase, heart in pilgrimage,
> The Christian plummet sounding Heav'n and earth;
> Engine against th' Almighty, sinners' tower,
> Reversed thunder, Christ-side-piercing spear,
> The six-days' world transposing in an hour,
> A kind of tune which all things hear and fear;
> Softness and peace, and joy and love and bliss,
> Exalted Manna, gladness of the best,
> Heaven in ordinary, man well drest,
> The milky way, the bird of paradise,
> Church bells beyond the stars heard, the soul's blood,
> The land of spices; something understood.
>
> George Herbert

So the poems in this selection have been chosen because of the vividness or potency or clarity with which they talk to God, as much as for their beauty; because they catch in a phrase or a line or a verse our experience of living at the same time in this world and beyond this world in constant relation to him. They are not simply religious reflections, or even ways of thinking about God, expressed by poets. They are prayers. That is, they are spoken to God himself, in wonder, delight, anger, fear and dereliction by men and women of great verbal artistry. They wrestle with him or plead with him or simply delight in him, in the skill of their craft. Always they have God at their centre, and view the darknesses and joys of our lives in relation to the one central and unchanging reality of our existence: that we are his creatures, living always within his will, and responding to life's circumstances from within that will. That is why they are truly prayers: because they engage with circumstances from within a life rooted in God, something quite different from engaging with God from a life drifting among circumstances. This distinction is a fundamental one, far more profound than differences of mood or even of faith and doubt. It showed itself very clearly in the Psalms, which are written out of just such a rooted-ness in the will of God, and which therefore can question and doubt him, rage and weep to him, as well as praise and rejoice in him, with complete freedom because they are living expressions of an organic and vital relationship.

This comparison with the Psalms suggests a way in which we might use this book. The poems are loosely grouped in six sections, which reflect the main contexts in which we talk to and listen to God. In the first section, of 'praise, adoration, thanksgiving' the poets simply look at God and pour out their wonder and delight and reverence. Sometimes they look at him as they know him in the created world: but even here they are delighting not simply in the freshness and wonder of Nature, but in the way those qualities reveal to us God himself. So, for instance, it is God's beauty, not simply that of the material world, which finally elicits delight in Gerard Manley Hopkins' 'Pied Beauty'. Alexander Pope put it finely, 'All are parts of one stupendous whole'.

But sometimes in this section the writers use no such intermediary to focus God's goodness, but praise him in direct adoration of his Being. Two such poets are amongst the earliest included, Caedmon and Cynewulf, in the poems 'Now we must praise the Ruler of Heaven', and 'Hail, heavenly beam, brightest of angels thou'. Others are caught up into the wonder of God as we know him in Jesus Christ, and burst out in astonishment or profound thankfulness with prayer-poems centred on God as Jesus, or on God's care for us in Jesus.

As a generation we are not good at this pure no-strings-attached contemplation, in love and awe and wonder, of our God. This is partly because it is the most selfless and least self-conscious prayer, requiring a willingness to stand back from our immediate needs and circumstances. Yet the glory of this kind of prayer is not only that it is the best offering we can possibly make, and therefore one we owe, to our Creator Father God. It is also that when we develop the daily habit of such prayer it is astonishing how differently we come to perceive what our needs and circumstances actually are. It might therefore be worth developing the practice of prefacing our use of prayers from any other section of the book with one from this group, to lead us into our own personal adoration and praise of God. The great gift of poets is often that of the striking or vivid phrase which can open to us a glimpse of this glory of God in a new or searching way.

This is not meant, however, to distance us from ordinary life. Quite the reverse: it is the context in which ordinary life is lived and talked over with God. So the second section is of 'prayer in the dailiness of life' and ranges from Robert Herrick's delightful 'Thanksgiving for his house', to Grace Nichol's 'Caribbean Woman Prayer', with its shrewd and yearning intercessions all mixed up with fervent praise bursting from her green and hibiscus land. The sense of being ordinary, and the struggle to be good, are offered and so become holy in the context of an entire world shot through with the holiness of God . . . 'O world invisible, we view thee . . .'

These are our everyday poem-prayers, for times when life flows on undramatically. But, inevitably, the lengthiest section is the third, where the poets talk to God in times of 'need, sorrow, sickness or any other adversity', and petition and intercession are interwoven with painful praise. Many of these face our deep sense of failure and sinfulness in the presence of a just God, and so are ways of expressing that we are sorry and ashamed; they give us the language to talk about this to God. Here, too, there is wondering praise to him for his forgiving, and its effect in our lives. This section also has prayers about the temptations we long to avoid, which circumstances may threaten us with: complacency, need, doubt, and finally despair.

This leads us to the way poets through the centuries have cried out to God in the greatest crisis of all, which all must face: that of dying. Poets as different as John Donne and Alfred Lord Tennyson, John Henry Newman and Emily Brontë, have found a way to speak directly to God of the agony of the death process, its mortal terror and its pain. Others like Henry Vaughan have expressed to God the anguish and perplexity of bereavement. It may be these will give words when our own praying has become voiceless with pain, words that can be directed to God in anger or terror or bitterness or bewilderment: images that express for us our grief at mortality.

There is prayer here, too, about the mystery of what follows death. Not all these are alight with longing for Heaven, and many may find great comfort in praying with Charlotte Mew's old shepherd not to lose for ever the dear places and sights and creatures of this world. Others make daring ventures of faith about what might be our future.

The liturgical context for such language is focussed in the great festivals of the Church, and so the fifth section points us to some of the 'Celebrations and Mysteries' we share as Christians, particularly those of Christmas and Easter. Here again we catch a sense of the different centuries crying to the same God in different languages; the same prayer, but understood so differently by Samuel Beckett and Edmund Spenser, Richard Crashaw and Kathleen Raine. Between them they speak to God of the pain as well as the glory of Christmas, of the immensity and yet the particularity of the events of Easter.

Beyond these events are the mysteries they represent, which are beyond our knowing. The last section gives tongue to this sense of 'not knowing', of 'Glimpses and Longings'. They touch on the mystery of the harshness with which God so often seems to treat his friends (Christina Rossetti's 'Twice'); the praying which breaks through the reasonable with a surge of power ('The prayer of Daft Harry'), Elizabeth Jennings' moving prayer not that God may be clearer but that she may be; and finally, the 'Journey Spell' with its hint of the mysterious power of incantation.

In using these prayers we become powerfully aware that here are men and women who think and yearn and praise as we do, but who have the gift to say it for us so that we know better what it is we want to say, or who can make the offering for us in a tongue we do not possess. In that sense poets serve one of the functions of the priest, in speaking for us. Yet far from leaving us lonely, with nothing to do before God, they bring us into great richness. For to pray with them is to be drawn from loneliness into the company of God, and of all God's people through time and space. It is to be drawn into the sweetness of intimate friendship, and yet the sweep and wonder of belonging to a great multitude, greater than we can number. It is to know our own small powers taken up and transformed beyond themselves, and returned to us for our use for God, clear and invigorated and swept clear of the need for personal recognition. It is to find that all that we have and are have found their right mode, and are at home in God's universe:

To be a stream in haste to join the ocean wide,
Lost within its depths. Evaporating then,
To fall as rain – refreshed, refreshing, clean.

To be a grain of sand, washed over by the tide,
Lost upon the shore. And then becoming firm,
The surface where God's footprints may be seen.

To be a note of music, pure melodic sound,
Lost in symphony. And then be played to blend
In harmony with orchestra divine.

To be a drop of glass, the Craftsman's rod wrapped round,
Lost within the fire. Then purified and shaped
Into the goblet for the heavenly wine.

To lose awareness, yet become the more aware –
This . . . this is prayer.

M. J. Norman

1 PRAISE, ADORATION, THANKSGIVING

Our Father in heaven, hallowed be your name

Wondering worship of the most high God – Man
to God in thankfulness – For love in creation

He whom I bow to only knows to whom I bow
When I attempt the ineffable Name, murmuring 'Thou'
And dream of Pheidian fancies and embrace in heart
Symbols (I know) which cannot be the thing Thou art.
Thus always, taken at their word, all prayers blaspheme
Worshipping with frail images a folk-lore dream,
And all men in their praying, self-deceived, address
The coinage of their own unquiet thoughts, unless
Thou in magnetic mercy to Thyself divert
Our arrows, aimed unskilfully, beyond desert;
And all men are idolators, crying unheard
To a deaf idol, if Thou take them at their word.

Take not, Oh Lord, our literal sense. Lord, in Thy great
Unbroken speech our limping metaphor translate.

C. S. Lewis

1. PRAISE, ADORATION, THANKSGIVING

Our Father in heaven, hallowed be your name

Hymn

Now we must praise the Ruler of Heaven,
The might of the Lord and his purpose of mind,
The work of the Glorious Father; for he
God Eternal, established each wonder,
He, Holy Creator, first fashioned the heavens
As a roof for the children of earth.
And then our Guardian, the Everlasting Lord,
Adorned this middle-earth for men.
Praise the Almighty King of Heaven.

Caedmon

Christic the Cornerstone

O King! Thou art the wall-stone,
which of old the workmen
from their work rejected!
Well it thee beseemeth
that thou hold the headship
of this Hall of glory,
and should'st join together
with a fastening firm
the broad-spaced walls
of the flint unbreakable
all fitly framed together;
that among earth's dwellers
all with sight of eyes
may for ever wonder.
O Prince of glory!
now through skill and wisdom
manifest thy handiwork,
true-fast and firm-set
   sovran splendour.

Based upon the antiphon *O Rex Gentium*

A Child my Choice

I praise him most, I love him best, all praise and love
   is his;
While him I love, in him I live, and cannot live amiss.

Love's sweetest mark, laud's highest theme, man's
   most desired light,
To love him life, to leave him death, to live in him
   delight.
He mine by gift, I his by debt, thus each to other due,
First friend he was, best friend he is, all times will try
   him true.

Though young, yet wise, though small, yet strong;
   though man, yet God he is;
As wise he knows, as strong he can, as God he loves
   to bless.
His knowledge rules, his strength defends, his love
   doth cherish all;
His birth our joy, his life our light, his death our end
   of thrall.

Robert Southwell

O Glorious God

Glorious the sun in mid career;
Glorious the assembled fires appear;
   Glorious the comet's train:
Glorious the trumpet and alarm;
Glorious the almighty stretched-out arm;
   Glorious the enraptured main:

Glorious the northern lights astream;
Glorious the song, when God's the theme
   Glorious the thunder's roar:
Glorious hosanna from the den;
Glorious the catholic amen;
   Glorious the martyr's gore:

Glorious – more glorious is the crown
Of him that brought salvation down
   By meekness called thy Son;
Thou that stupendous truth believed,
And now the matchless deed's achieved,
   DETERMINED, DARED, and DONE.

Christopher Smart

Veni Creator Spiritus

Creator Spirit, by whose aid
The world's foundations first were laid,
Come visit every pious mind;
Come pour thy joys on humankind;
From sin and sorrow set us free,
And make thy temples worthy thee . . .

Plenteous of grace, descend from high,
Rich in thy sevenfold energy,
Thou strength of his almighty hand,
Whose power does heaven and earth command!
Proceeding Spirit, our defence,
Who dost the gift of tongues dispense,
And crown'st thy gift with eloquence!

Refine and purge our earthy parts;
But, O, inflame and fire our hearts!
Our frailties help, our vice control,
Submit the senses to the soul;
And when rebellious they are grown,
Then lay thy hand and hold them down.

Chase from our minds the infernal foe,
And peace, the fruit of love, bestow;
And lest our feet should step astray,
Protect and guide us in the way.

Make us eternal truths receive,
And practise all that we believe:
Give us thyself that we may see
The Father and the Son, by thee.

Immortal honour, endless fame,
Attend the Almighty Father's Name:
The Saviour Son be glorified,
Who for lost man's redemption died;
And equal adoration be,
Eternal Paraclete, to thee.

John Dryden

Lovest Thou Me?

Hark, my soul! it is the Lord;
'Tis thy Saviour, hear his word;
Jesus speaks, and speaks to thee:
'Say, poor sinner, lov'st thou me?

I delivered thee when bound,
And, when wounded, healed thy wound;
Sought thee wandering, set thee right,
Turned thy darkness into light.

Can a woman's tender care
Cease towards the child she bare?
Yes, she may forgetful be,
Yet will I remember thee.

Mine is an unchanging love,
Higher than the heights above;
Deeper than the depths beneath,
Free and faithful, strong as death.

Thou shalt see my glory soon,
When the work of grace is done;
Partner of my throne shalt be;
Say, poor sinner, lov'st thou me?'

Lord, it is my chief complaint
That my love is weak and faint;
Yet I love thee and adore,
Oh for grace to love thee more!

William Cowper

Over wrath grace shall abound

O goodness infinite, goodness immense!
That all this good of evil shall produce,
And evil turn to good; more wonderful
Than that which by creation first brought forth
Light out of darkness! Full of doubt I stand,
Whether I should repent me now of sin
By me done and occasioned, or rejoice
Much more, that much more good thereof shall
    spring,
To God more glory, more good will to men
From God, and over wrath grace shall abound . . .
Henceforth I learn that to obey is best,
And love with fear the only God, to walk
As in his presence, ever to observe
His providence, and on him sole depend,
Merciful over all his works, with good
Still overcoming evil, and by small
Accomplishing great things, by things deemed weak
Subverting worldly strong, and worldly wise
By simply meek; that suffering for truth's sake
Is fortitude to highest victory,
And to the faithful death the gate of life;
Taught this by his example whom I now
Acknowledge my Redeemer ever blest.

John Milton

The Flower

How fresh, O Lord, how sweet and clean
Are thy returns! ev'n as the flowers in spring;
   To which, besides their own demean,
The late-past frosts tributes of pleasure bring.
     Grief melts away
     Like snow in May,
As if there were no such cold thing.

Who would have thought my shrivel'd heart
Could have recover'd greenness? It was gone
   Quite under ground; as flowers depart
To see their mother-root, when they have blown;
     Where they together
     All the hard weather,
Dead to the world, keep house unknown.

These are thy wonders, Lord of power,
Killing and quickening, bringing down to hell
   And up to heaven in an hour;
Making a chiming of a passing-bell.
     We say amiss,
     This or that is:
Thy word is all, if we could spell.

O that I once past changing were,
Fast in thy Paradise, where no flower can wither!
   Many a spring I shoot up fair,
Off'ring at heav'n, growing and groaning thither:
     Nor doth my flower
     Want a spring shower,
My sins and I joining together . . .

And now in age I bud again,
After so many deaths I live and write;
  I once more smell the dew and rain,
And relish versing: O my only light,
    It cannot be
    That I am he
On whom thy tempests fell all night.

These are thy wonders, Lord of love,
To make us see we are but flowers that glide:
  Which when we once can find and prove,
Thou hast a garden for us, where to bide.
    Who would be more,
    Swelling through store,
Forefeit their Paradise by their pride.

George Herbert

A Hymn of Love

Ay me, dear Lord, that ever I might hope,
For all the pains and woes that I endure,
To come at length unto the wished scope
Of my desire; or might my self assure,
That happy port for ever to recure.
Then would I think these pains no pains at all,
And all my woes to be but penance small.

Then would I sing of thine immortal praise
An heavenly Hymn, such as the Angels sing,
And thy triumphant name then would I raise
'Bove all the gods, thee only honouring,
My guide, my God, my victor, and my king;
Till then, dread Lord, vouchsafe to take of me
This simple song, thus fram'd in praise of thee.

Edmund Spenser

To Christ our Lord

Hail, heavenly beam, brightest of angels thou,
sent unto men upon this middle-earth!
Thou art the true refulgence of the sun,
radiant above the stars, and from thyself
illuminest for ever all the tides of time.
And as thou, God indeed begotten of God,
thou Son of the true Father, wast from aye,
without beginning, in the heaven's glory,
so now thy handiwork in its sore need
prayeth thee boldly that thou send to us
the radiant sun, and that thou comest thyself
to enlighten those who for so long a time
were wrapt around with darkness, and here in gloom
have sat the livelong night, shrouded in sin.

Cynewulf

Ode

The spacious firmament on high
With all the blue ethereal sky,
And spangled heavens, a shining frame,
Their great Original proclaim:
The unwearied sun, from day to day,
Does his Creator's power display,
And publishes to every land
The work of an almighty hand.

Soon as the evening shades prevail,
The moon takes up the wondrous tale,
And nightly to the listening earth
Repeats the story of her birth:
Whilst all the stars that round her burn,
And all the planets in their turn,
Confirm the tidings as they roll,
And spread the truth from pole to pole.

What though, in solemn silence, all
Move round the dark, terrestrial ball?
What though nor real voice nor sound
Amid their radiant orbs be found?
In reason's ear they all rejoice,
And utter forth a glorious voice,
For ever singing, as they shine,
'The hand that made us is divine.'

Joseph Addison

Dust

Sweet sovereign Lord of this so pined-for Spring,
How breathe the homage of but one poor heart
With such small compass of thy everything?

Ev'n though I knew this were my life's last hour,
It yet would lie, past hope, beyond my power
One instant of my gratitude to prove,
My praise, my love.

That 'Everything'! – when this, my human dust,
Whereto return I must,
Were scant to bring to bloom a single flower!

Walter de la Mare

If I Take The Wings Of The Morning

taking off at dawn
to circle *ultima thule*,

threading the splendours between
ice and pearl cloud cover,

God is not only also
there, but signally there,

who made the heavens skilfully,
who made the great lights
with a strong hand and a strained-out arm,

who brought forth clouds from the end of the world
and sent forth lightnings with rain
and out of his treasuries high winds.

When those who keep us in prison
ask of us mirth in our hang-ups
with 'Sing us a song of Zion',
what can we sing or say
under the mourning willows
of a common suffering in
the river-meadows of Babel?

It is our lingo utters us, not we.
Our native tongue, our endowment,
determines what we can say.
And who endowed us?

Speak if you cannot sing.
Utter with appropriate shudders
the extremities of God's arctic
when all the rivers are frozen,

and how He tempers our exile
with an undeserved planting of willows.

Donald Davie

Bermudas

Where the remote Bermudas ride
In the ocean's bosom unespied,
From a small boat, that rowed along,
The listening winds received this song.

   'What should we do but sing his praise
That led us through the watery maze,
Unto an isle so long unknown,
And yet far kinder than our own?

Where he the huge sea-monsters wracks,
That lift the deep upon their backs.
He lands us on a grassy stage;
Safe from the storms, and prelate's rage.

He gave us this eternal spring,
Which here enamels everything,
And sends the fowl to us in care,
On daily visits through the air.

He hangs in shades the orange bright,
Like golden lamps in a green night,
And does in the pom'granates close
Jewels more rich than Ormus shows.

He makes the figs our mouths to meet,
And throws the melons at our feet,
But apples plants of such a price,
No tree could ever bear them twice . . .

He cast (of which we rather boast)
The gospel's pearl upon our coast,
And in these rocks for us did frame
A temple, where to sound his name.

Oh let our voice his praise exalt,
Till it arrive at heaven's vault:
Which thence (perhaps) rebounding, may
Echo beyond the Mexique Bay.'

    Thus sung they, in the English boat,
An holy and a cheerful note,
And all the way, to guide their chime,
With falling oars they kept the time.

Andrew Marvell

Pied Beauty

Glory be to God for dappled things –
    For skies of couple-colour as a brinded cow;
      For rose-moles all in stipple upon trout that
        swim;
Fresh-firecoal chestnut-falls; finches' wings;
    Landscape plotted and pieced – fold, fallow, and
      plough
      And áll trádes, their gear and tackle and trim.

All things counter, original, spare, strange;
    Whatever is fickle freckled (who knows how?)
      With swift, slow; sweet, sour; adazzle, dim;
He fathers-forth whose beauty is past change:
                  Praise him.

Gerard Manley Hopkins

Wholeness

What if the foot, ordain'd the dust to tread,
Or hand, to toil, aspired to be the head?
What if the head, the eye, or ear repined
To serve mere engines to the ruling mind?
Just as absurd for any part to claim
To be another, in this general frame;
Just as absurd, to mourn the tasks or pains
The great Directing Mind of all ordains.
All are but parts of one stupendous whole,
Whose body Nature is, and God the soul;
That, changed through all, and yet in all the same;
Great in the earth, as in the ethereal frame;
Warms in the sun, refreshes in the breeze,
Glows in the stars, and blossoms in the trees;
Lives through all life, extends through all extent;
Spreads undivided, operates unspent!
Breathes in our soul, informs our mortal part,
As full, as perfect, in a hair as heart;
As full, as perfect in vile man that mourns,
As the rapt seraph that adores and burns;
To him no high, no low, no great, no small;
He fills, He bounds, connects, and equals all.

Alexander Pope

Joy and peace in believing

Sometimes a light surprises
    The Christian while he sings;
It is the Lord who rises
    With healing in his wings:
When comforts are declining,
    He grants the soul again
A season of clear shining,
    To cheer it after rain.

In holy contemplation,
    We sweetly then pursue
The theme of God's salvation,
    And find it ever new;
Set free from present sorrow,
    We cheerfully can say,
E'en let the unknown tomorrow
    Bring with it what it may.

It can bring with it nothing,
    But he will bear us through;
Who gives the lilies clothing,
    Will clothe his people too;
Beneath the spreading heavens
    No creature but is fed;
And he who feeds the ravens
    Will give his children bread.

Though vine nor fig tree neither
    Their wonted fruit shall bear,
Though all the field should wither,
    Nor flocks nor herds be there:
Yet God the same abiding,
    His praise shall tune my voice;
For, while in him confiding,
    I cannot but rejoice.

William Cowper

An Hymn

When all thy mercies, O my God,
  My rising soul surveys,
Transported with the view, I'm lost
  In wonder, love and praise . . .

Thy Providence my life sustain'd,
  And all my wants redrest;
When in the silent womb I lay,
  And hung upon the breast . . .

Unnumber'd comforts to my soul
  Thy tender care bestow'd,
Before my infant heart conceiv'd
  From whence those comforts flow'd.

When in the slippery paths of youth
  With heedless steps I ran,
Thine arm unseen convey'd me safe,
  And led me up to man . . .

When worn with sickness, oft hast thou
  With health renew'd my face;
And when in sins and sorrow sunk,
  Reviv'd my soul with grace.

Thy bounteous hand with worldly bliss
  Has made my cup run o'er,
And in a kind and faithful friend
  Hast doubled all my store . . .

Through every period of my life
  Thy goodness I'll pursue,
And after death, in distant worlds,
  The glorious theme renew . . .

Through all eternity to thee
  A joyful song I'll raise;
But oh! eternity's too short
  To utter all thy praise.

Joseph Addison

2. PRAYER IN THE DAILINESS OF LIFE

Your kingdom come, your will be done, on earth as in heaven; give us today our daily bread

God who is our Way – On being very ordinary – On trying to be good each day – To God who is in the world – And in the evening

More things are wrought by prayer
Than this world dreams of. Wherefore, let thy voice
Rise like a fountain for me night and day.
For what are men better than sheep or goats
That nourish a blind life within the brain,
If, knowing God, they lift not hands of prayer
Both for themselves and those who call them friend?

For so the whole round earth is every way
Bound by gold chains about the feet of God.

Alfred Lord Tennyson

The Call

Come, my Way, my Truth, my Life:
Such a Way, as gives us breath:
Such a Truth, as ends all strife:
Such a Life, as killeth death.

Come, my Light, my Feast, my Strength:
Such a Light, as shows a feast:
Such a Feast, as mends in length:
Such a Strength, as makes his guest.

Come my Joy, my Love, my Heart:
Such a Joy, as none can move:
Such a Love, as none can part:
Such a Heart, as joys in love.

George Herbert

Be the power of all things within us

O God the Holy Ghost who art Light
    unto thine elect,
  Evermore enlighten us.
Thou who art Fire of Love,
  Evermore enkindle us.
Thou who art Lord and Giver of Life,
  Evermore live in us.
Thou who bestowest sevenfold grace,
  Evermore replenish us.
As the wind is thy symbol,
  So forward our goings.
As the dove,
  So launch us heavenwards.
As water,
  So purify our spirits.
As a cloud,
  So abate our temptations.
As dew,
  So revive our languor.
As fire,
  So purge out our dross.

Christina Rossetti

My way, my life, my light

'Wherefore hidest thou thy face?' Job 13.24.

Why dost Thou shade Thy lovely face? O why
Does that eclipsing hand so long deny
The sunshine of Thy soul-enlivening eye?

Without that Light, what light remains in me?
Thou art my Life, my Way, my Light; in Thee
I live, I move, and by Thy beams I see.

Thou art my Life: if Thou but turn away,
My life's a thousand deaths: Thou art my Way;
Without Thee, Lord, I travel not, but stray.

My Light Thou art; without Thy glorious sight,
Mine eyes are darkened with perpetual night.
My God, Thou art my Way, my Life, my Light.

Thou art my Way; I wander, if Thou fly:
Thou art my Light; if hid, how blind am I!
Thou art my Life; if thou withdraw, I die.

Mine eyes are blind and dark, I cannot see;
To whom, or whither, should my darkness flee,
But to the Light? And who's that Light but Thee?

My path is lost; my wandering steps do stray;
I cannot safely go, nor safely stay;
Whom should I seek but Thee, my Path, my Way?

*   *   *   *   *

Thou art the pilgrim's Path; the blind man's Eye;
The dead man's Life; on Thee my hopes rely;
If Thou remove, I err, I grope, I die.

Disclose Thy sunbeams; close Thy wings, and stay:
See, see how I am blind, and dead, and stray,
O Thou, that art my Light, my Life, my Way.

Francis Quarles

Contentment

He that is down needs fear no fall;
    He that is low, no pride;
He that is humble, ever shall
    Have God to be his guide.
I am content with what I have,
    Little be it, or much:
And, Lord, contentment still I crave,
    Because thou savest such.

John Bunyan

A Thanksgiving to God for His House

Lord, thou hast given me a cell
    Wherein to dwell;
A little house, whose humble roof
    Is weather-proof . . .
Low is my porch, as is my fate,
    Both void of state;
And yet the threshold of my door
    Is worn by th' poor,
Who thither come, and freely get
    Good words or meat;
Like as my parlour, so my hall
    And kitchen's small;
A little buttery, and therein
    A little bin
Which keeps my little loaf of bread
    Unclipped, unflead.
Some brittle sticks of thorn or briar
    Make me a fire,
Close by whose living coal I sit,
    And glow like it.
Lord, I confess, too, when I dine,
    The pulse is thine,
And all those other bits, that be
    There placed by thee . . .
Lord, 'tis thy plenty-dropping hand,
    That soils my land;
And giv'st me for my bushel sown,
    Twice ten for one.
Thou mak'st my teeming hen to lay
    Her egg each day;
Besides my healthful ewes to bear
    Me twins each year,
The while the conduits of my kine
    Run cream for wine.

All these, and better thou dost send
    Me, to this end,
That I should render, for my part,
    A thankful heart;
Which, fired with incense, I resign,
    As wholly thine;
But the acceptance, that must be,
    My Christ, by thee.

Robert Herrick

What more doth the Lord require of thee?

To love our God with all our strength and will;
To covet nothing; to devise no ill
Against our neighbours; to procure or do
Nothing to others which we would not to
Our very selves; not to revenge our wrong;
To be content with little; not to long
For wealth and greatness; to despise or jeer
No man, and, if we be despised, to bear;
To feed the hungry; to hold fast our crown;
To take from others nought; to give our own, –
These are his precepts, and, alas, in these
What is so hard but faith can do with ease?

Henry Vaughan

'Good Lord, Deliver us!'

From being anxious, or secure,
Dead clods of sadness, or light squibs of mirth,
  From thinking that great courts immure
All, or no happiness, or that this earth
    Is only for our prison framed,
    Or that thou art covetous
To them whom thou lov'st, or that they are maimed
From reaching this world's sweet who seek thee thus
With all their might, good Lord, deliver us.

  From needing danger to be good,
From owing thee yesterday's tears today,
  From trusting so much to thy blood
That in that hope we wound our souls away,
    From bribing thee with alms to excuse
    Some sin more burdenous,
From light affecting, in religion, news,
From thinking us all soul, neglecting thus
Our mutual duties, Lord, deliver us . . .

  When senses, which thy soldiers are,
We arm against thee, and they fight for sin,
  When want, sent but to tame, doth war
And work despair a breach to enter in,
    When plenty, God's image and seal,
    Makes us idolatrous,
And love it, not him, whom it should reveal,
When we are moved to seem religious
Only to vent wit, Lord deliver us.

John Donne

Hymn for the Church Militant

Great God, that bowest sky and star,
    Bow down our towering thoughts to thee,
And grant us in a faltering war
    The firm feet of humility.

Lord, we that snatch the swords of flame,
    Lord, we that cry about thy ear,
We too are weak with pride and shame,
    We too are as our foemen are.

Yea, we are mad as they are mad,
    Yea, we are blind as they are blind,
Yea, we are very sick and sad
    Who bring good news to all mankind.

The dreadful joy thy Son has sent
    Is heavier than any care;
We find, as Cain his punishment,
    Our pardon more than we can bear.

Lord, when we cry thee far and near
    And thunder through all lands unknown
The gospel into every ear,
    Lord, let us not forget our own.

Cleanse us from ire of creed or class,
    The anger of the idle kings;
Sow in our souls, like living grass,
    The laughter of all lowly things.

G. K. Chesterton

Student Taper

When
– At the mid of moon,
At end of day –
My lamp is lit,
Grant me a boon,
I pray,
And do
So order it

– That the small creatures,
Terrified and blind;
The gold and silvern moths
Of lovely kind,
Do not whirl to my taper,
Nor, therein,
Die, painfully,
And bring my light
To sin.

My light
is innocent!
Grant
– That it may be
Harmless,
And helpful,
And remarked
Of thee.

James Stephens

Self-acquaintance

Dear Lord! accept a sinful heart,
  Which of itself complains,
And mourns, with much and frequent smart,
The evil it contains.

There fiery seeds of anger lurk,
  Which often hurt my frame;
And wait but for the tempter's work,
  To fan them to a flame.

Legality holds out a bribe
  To purchase life from thee;
And discontent would fain prescribe
  How thou shalt deal with me.

While unbelief withstands thy grace,
  And puts the mercy by;
Presumption, with a brow of brass,
  Says, 'Give me, or I die.'

How eager are my thoughts to roam
  In quest of what they love!
But ah! when duty calls them home,
  How heavily they move!

Oh! cleanse me in a Saviour's blood,
  Transform me by thy power,
And make me thy beloved abode,
  And let me rove no more.

William Cowper

Caribbean Woman Prayer

Wake up Lord
brush de sunflakes from yuh eye
back de sky a while Lord
an hear dis Mother-woman
on behalf of her pressure-down people

God de Mudder
God de Fadder
God de Sister
God de Brudder
God de Holy Fire

Ah don't need to tell yuh
how tings stan
cause right now you know
dat old lizard ah walk
lick land
an you know how de pickney belly laang
an you know how de fork ah hit stone
an tho it rain you know it really drought
an even now de man have start fuh count

de wata he make

God de Fadder
God de Mudder
God de Sister
God de Brudder
God de Holy Fire

Give me faith

O Lord
you know we is ah people
of a proud an generous heart

and how it shame us bad
dat we kyant welcome friend or stranger
when eat time come around

You know is not we nature
to behave like yard fowl

You know dat is de politics
an de times
an de tricks
dat has reduced we to dis

An talking bout politics Lord
I hope you give de politicians dem
de courage to do what they have to do
an to mek dem see dat tings must grow
from within
an not from without
even as you suffer us not
to walk in de rags of doubt

Mek dem see dat de people
must be at de root of de heart
dat dis place ain't Uncle Sam backyard
Lord, look how Rodney and Bishop get blast

God de Mudder
God de Fadder
God de Sister
God de Brudder
God de Holy Fire

To cut a laang story short
I want to see de children
wake up happy to de sunrise
an food in de pot

I want to see dem stretch limb
an watch dem sleep pon good stomach

40

I want to see de loss of hope
everywhere replace
wid de win of living

I want to see de man an woman
being in they being

Yes Lord
Halleliuh Lord!

All green tings an hibiscus praises Lord

Grace Nichols

The Kingdom of God

O World invisible, we view thee,
O World intangible, we touch thee,
O World unknowable, we know thee,
Inapprehensible, we clutch thee!

Does the fish soar to find the ocean,
The eagle plunge to find the air –
That we ask of the stars in motion
If they have rumour of thee there?

Not where the wheeling systems darken,
And our benumbed conceiving soars! –
The drift of pinions, would we hearken,
Beats at our own clay-shuttered doors.

The angels keep their ancient places; –
Turn but a stone, and start a wing!
'Tis ye, 'tis your estrangèd faces,
That miss the many-splendoured thing.

But (when so sad thou canst not sadder)
Cry; – and upon thy so sore loss
Shall shine the traffic of Jacob's ladder
Pitched betwixt Heaven and Charing Cross.

Yea, in the night, my Soul, my daughter,
Cry, – clinging Heaven by the hems;
And lo, Christ walking on the water,
Not of Genesareth, but Thames!

Francis Thompson

The Everlasting Mercy

O wet red swathe of earth laid bare,
O truth, O strength, O gleaming share,
O patient eyes that watch the goal,
O ploughman of the sinner's soul,
O Jesus, drive the coulter deep
To plough my living man from sleep.

O Christ who holds the open gate,
O Christ who drives the furrow straight,
O Christ, the plough, O Christ, the laughter
Of holy white birds flying after,
Lo, all my heart's field red and torn,
And thou wilt bring the young green corn,
The young green corn divinely springing,
The young green corn for ever singing;
And when the field is fresh and fair
Thy blessèd feet shall glitter there.
And we will walk the weeded field,
And tell the golden harvest's yield,
The corn that makes the holy bread
By which the soul of man is fed,
The holy bread, the food unpriced,
Thy everlasting mercy, Christ.

John Masefield

Evening prayer

Oh, thou that art unwearying, that dost neither sleep
   Not slumber, who didst take
All care for Lazarus in the careless tomb, oh keep
   Watch for me till I wake.
If thou think for me what I cannot think, if thou
   Desire for me what I
Cannot desire, my soul's interior Form, though now
   Deep-buried, will not die,
– No more than the insensible dropp'd seed which
     grows
   Through winter ripe for birth
Because, while it forgets, the heaven remembering
     throws
   Sweet influence still on earth,
– Because the heaven, moved moth-like by thy
     beauty, goes
   Still turning round the earth.

C. S. Lewis

3. IN NEED, SORROW, SICKNESS OR ANY OTHER ADVERSITY

Forgive us our sins as we forgive those who sin against us; and lead us not into temptation

The angry Lord – On being penitent – On failure and repeated sin – On the completeness of God's forgiveness – Lead us not into complacency; despair; doubt; need – 'God who knows all his sheep shall all in safety keep.'

Prayer yet could be a dance
But still a cross. I offer small heartbreak
Catch grace almost by chance.

Elizabeth Jennings

Where is your relief?

No worst, there is none. Pitched past pitch of grief,
More pangs will, schooled at forepangs, wilder
   wring.
Comforter, where, where is your comforting?
Mary, mother of us, where is your relief?
My cries heave, herds-long; huddle in a main, a chief
Woe, wórld-sorrow; on an áge-old anvil wince and
   sing –
Then lull, then leave off. Fury had shrieked 'No ling-
ering! Let me be fell: force I must be brief'.

O the mind, mind has mountains; cliffs of fall
Frightful, sheer, no-man-fathomed. Hold them cheap
May who ne'er hung there. Nor does long our small
Durance deal with that steep or deep. Here! creep,
Wretch, under a comfort serves in a whirlwind: all
Life death does end and each day dies with sleep.

Gerard Manley Hopkins

47

Litany to the Holy Spirit

In the hour of my distress,
When temptations me oppress,
And when I my sins confess,
    Sweet Spirit, comfort me!

When I lie within my bed,
Sick in heart and sick in head,
And with doubts discomforted,
    Sweet Spirit, comfort me!

When the house doth sigh and weep,
And the world is drowned in sleep,
Yet mine eyes the watch do keep,
    Sweet Spirit, comfort me! . . .

When the passing bell doth toll,
And the furies in a shoal
Come to fright a parting soul,
    Sweet Spirit, comfort me!

When the tapers now burn blue,
And the comforters are few,
And that number more than true,
    Sweet Spirit, comfort me! . . .

When, God knows, I'm tossed about,
Either with despair, or doubt;
Yet before the glass be out,
    Sweet Spirit, comfort me! . . .

When the judgement is revealed,
And that opened which was sealed,
When to thee I have appealed,
    Sweet Spirit, comfort me!

Robert Herrick

'My spirit longeth for thee'

My spirit longeth for thee
   Within my troubled breast;
Although I be unworthy
   Of so divine a Guest.

Of so divine a Guest,
   Unworthy though I be;
Yet has my heart no rest,
   Unless it come from thee.

Unless it come from thee,
   In vain I look around;
In all that I can see,
   No rest is to be found.

No rest is to be found,
   But in thy blessed love;
O, let my wish be crowned,
   And send it from above.

John Byrom

'Moon-like is all other love'

Moon-like is all other love:
First crescent, then decreasing, gain;
Flower that buds, and soon goes off;
A day that fleets away in rain.

All other love bravely starts out,
But ends with torture, and in tears;
No love can salve the torment out
But that the King of Heaven bears:

For ever springing, ever new,
For ever the full orb, it is
A thing not thinned, from which accrue
Always new sweets, new centuries.

For this love, I all others fled:
Tell me where you may be found!
'Meek Mary is one fountainhead;
But Christ, Christ rather, is the ground.'

I did not find you, Christ found me.
Hold me, hold me fast, or else,
For all that that love steadfast be,
This love of mine swerves as it swells.

And yet, and yet – I *hurt*, the blood
Floods from my heart. My God, I see,
Leaves me in this. So, well and good . . .
Yet still I pray: 'God be with me.'

Alas, what should I do in Rome?
I take a leaf from carnal love:
No mortal troth dare I trust home
Except he help that sits above.

Anonymous, 14th century, translated by Donald Davie

Comfort me, Saviour

Speak low to me, my Saviour, low and sweet
From out the hallelujahs, sweet and low,
Lest I should fear and fall, and miss thee so
Who art not missed by any that entreat.
Speak to me as to Mary at thy feet!
And if no precious gums my hands bestow,
Let my tears drop like amber, while I go
In reach of thy divinest voice complete
In humanest affection – thus, in sooth,
To lose the sense of losing. As a child,
Whose song-bird seeks the wood for evermore,
Is sung to in its stead by mother's mouth
Till, sinking on her breast, love-reconciled,
He sleeps the faster that he wept before.

Elizabeth Barrett Browning

A prayer for our Church

My God, when I walk in those groves
And leaves thy spirit doth still fan,
I see in each shade that there grows
An angel talking with a man.

Under a juniper some house,
Or the cool myrtle's canopy,
Others beneath an oak's green boughs,
Or at some fountain's bubbling eye;

Here Jacob dreams and wrestles; there
Elias by a raven is fed,
Another time by the angel, where
He brings him water with his bread; . . .

Nay, thou thyself, my God, in fire,
Whirlwinds, and clouds, and the soft voice
Speak'st there so much, that I admire
We have no conference in these days.

Is the truce broke? or 'cause we have
A mediator now with thee,
Dost thou therefore old treaties waive
And by appeals from him decree?

Or is't so, as some green heads say
That now all miracles must cease?
Though thou hast promised they should stay
The tokens of the Church, and peace.

No, no; religion is a spring
That from some secret, golden mine
Derives her birth, and thence doth bring
Cordials in every drop, and wine;

But in her long and hidden course
Passing through the earth's dark veins,
Grows still from better unto worse,
And both her taste and colour stains . . .

Heal then these waters, Lord; or bring thy flock,
Since these are troubled, to the springing rock,
Look down, great Master of the Feast; O shine,
And turn once more our water into wine!

Henry Vaughan

Thanksgiving

We give thanks for St Thomas,
   All we who have known
   The darkness of disbelief,
The hollowness at the heart of Christmas,
The intolerable emptiness of Easter,
   The grief of separation.

With thy great mercy thou dost enfold us,
The waverers, the aliens, who stood apart, alone.
   For the impoverishments of our barren years
     Thou wilt atone.

Now with the faithful company we bring,
From depths of thankfulness
   Our adoration
    To thee,
   O, Christ our King.

Edith Forrest

The Prayer of a Modern Thomas

If Thou, O God, the Christ didst leave,
In Him, not Thee, I do believe;
   To Jesus dying all alone,
   To His dark Cross, not Thy bright Throne,
My hopeless hands will cleave.

But if it was Thy love that died,
Thy voice that in the darkness cried,
   The print of nails I long to see,
   In Thy hands, God, who fashioned me.
Show me *Thy* piercèd side.

Edward Shillito

Dost thou touch me afresh?

Thou mastering me
God! giver of breath and bread;
World's strand, sway of the sea;
Lord of living and dead;
Thou hast bound bones and veins in me, fastened me
fresh,
And after it almost unmade, what with dread,
Thy doing: and dost thou touch me afresh?
Over again I feel thy finger and find thee.

I did say yes
O at lightning and lashed rod;
Thou heardst me truer than tongue confess
Thy terror, O Christ, O God;
Thou knowest the walls, altar, and hour and night:
The swoon of a heart that the sweep and the hurl of
thee trod
Hard down with a horror of height:
And the midriff astrain with leaning of, laced with
fire of stress.

Gerard Manley Hopkins

The Contrite Heart

The Lord will happiness divine
   On contrite hearts bestow;
Then tell me, gracious God, is mine
   A contrite heart or no?

I hear, but seem to hear in vain,
   Insensible as steel;
If aught is felt, 'tis only pain,
   To find I cannot feel.

I sometimes think myself inclined
   To love thee, if I could;
But often feel another mind,
   Averse to all that's good.

My best desires are faint and few,
   I fain would strive for more;
But when I cry, 'My strength renew!'
   Seem weaker than before.

Thy saints are comforted, I know,
   And love thy house of prayer;
I therefore go where others go,
   But find no comfort there.

Oh! make this heart rejoice or ache;
   Decide this doubt for me;
And if it be not broken, break,
   And heal it, if it be.

William Cowper

Thee alone my hopes attend

Out of my soul's depth to thee my cries have
   sounded:
Let thine ears my plaints receive, on just fear
   grounded.
Lord, should'st thou weigh our faults, who's not
   confounded?

But with grace thou censur'st thine when they have
   errèd,
Therefore shall thy blessed named be loved and
   fearèd.
E'en to thy throne my thoughts and eyes are rearèd.

Thee alone my hopes attend, on thee relying;
In thy sacred word I'll trust, to thee fast flying,
Long ere the watch shall break, the morn descrying.

In the mercies of our God who live securèd,
May of full redemption rest in him assurèd,
Their sin-sick souls by him shall be recurèd.

Thomas Campion

De profundis clamavi
A version of Psalm 130

From depth of sin and from a deep despair,
   From depth of death, from depth of heart's sorrow,
   From this deep Cave of darkness, deep repair,
Thee have I called, O Lord, to be my borrow;
   Thou in my voice, O Lord, perceive and hear
   My heart, my hope, my plaint, my overthrow,
My will to rise: and let by grant of fear
   That to my voice thine ears do well attend.
   No place so far that to thee is not near;
No depth so deep that thou ne mayest extend
   Thine ear thereto: hear then my woeful plaint.
   For, Lord, if thou do observe what men offend
And put thy native mercy in restraint,
   If just exaction demand recompense,
   Who may endure, O Lord? Who shall not faint
At such account? Dread, and not reverence
   Should so rain large. But thou seek'st rather love.
   For in thy hand is mercy's residence,
By hope whereof thou dost our heartès move.
   I in thee, Lord, have set my confidence;
   My soul such trust doth evermore approve.
Thy holy word of eterne excellence,
   Thy mercy's promise that is alway just,
   Have been my stay, my pillar and pretence.
My soul in God hath more desirous trust
   Than hath the watchman looking for the day,
   By the relief to quench of sleep the thrust.
Let Israel trust unto the Lord alway,
   For grace and favour are his property;
   Plenteous ransome shall come with him, I say,
And shall redeem all our iniquity.

Sir Thomas Wyatt

Help, Good Shepherd

Turn not aside, Shepherd, to see
How bright the constellations are,
Hanging in heaven, or on the tree;
The skyborn or terrestrial star

Brood not upon; the waters fleet,
Willows, or thy crown-destined thorn,
Full of her rubies, as is meet,
Or whitening in the eye of morn,

Pause not beside: Shepherds' delight,
The pipe and tabor in the vale,
And mirthful watchfires of a night,
And herdsman's rest in wattled pale,

Forsake, though deeply earned: and still
Sound with thy crook the darkling flood,
Still range the sides of shelvy hill
And call about in underwood:

For on the hill are many strayed,
Some held in thickets plunge and cry,
And the deep waters make us afraid.
Come then and help us, or we die.

Ruth Pitter

Denial

When my devotions could not pierce
                Thy silent ears;
Then was my heart broken, as was my verse;
  My breast was full of fears,
                    And disorder.

My bent thoughts, like a brittle bow,
                Did fly asunder:
Each took his way; some would to pleasure go,
  Some to the wars and thunder
                  Of alarms.

As good go anywhere, they say,
                As to benumb
Both knees and heart, in crying night and day,
  Come, come, my God, O come,
                  But no hearing.

O that thou shouldst give dust a tongue
                To cry to thee,
And then not hear it crying! all day long
  My heart was in my knee,
                  But no hearing.

Therefore my soul lay out of sight,
                Untuned, unstrung;
My feeble spirit, unable to look right,
  Like a nipped blossom, hung
                  Discontented.

O cheer and tune my heartless breast,
                         Defer no time;
That so thy favours granting my request,
       They and my mind may chime,
                         And mend my rhyme.

George Herbert

God help me with myself

God strengthen me to bear myself;
That heaviest weight of all to bear,
Inalienable weight of care . . .

If I could once lay down myself,
And start self-purged upon the race
That all must run! Death runs apace.

If I could set aside myself,
And start with lightened heart upon
The road by all men overgone!

God harden me against myself,
This coward with pathetic voice
Who craves for ease, and rest and joys:

Myself, arch-traitor to myself,
My hollowest friend, my deadliest foe
My clog whatever road I go.

Yet One there is can curb myself,
Can roll the strangling load from me,
Break off the yoke and set me free.

Christina Rossetti

A version of Psalm 6

Lord, in thine anger do not reprehend me,
  Nor in thy hot displeasure me correct;
Pity me, Lord, for I am much deject,
  Am very weak and faint; heal and amend me,
For all my bones, that even with anguish ache,
  Are troubled, yea, my soul is troubled sore.
And thou, O Lord, how long? turn, Lord, restore
  My soul, O save me for thy goodness sake,
For in death no remembrance is of thee;
  Who in the grave can celebrate thy praise?
Wearied I am with sighing out my days,
  Nightly my couch I make a kind of sea;
My bed I water with my tears; mine eye
  Through grief consumes, is waxen old and dark
I' th' midst of all mine enemies that mark.
  Depart, all ye that work iniquity.
Depart from me, for the voice of my weeping
  The Lord hath heard; the Lord hath heard my
     prayer;
My supplication with acceptance fair
  The Lord will own, and have me in his keeping.
Mine enemies shall all be blank and dashed
  With much confusion; then grow red with shame;
They shall return in haste the way they came
  And in a moment shall be quite abashed.

John Milton

Bitter-Sweet

Ah my dear angry Lord,
Since thou dost love, yet strike;
Cast down, yet help afford;
Sure I will do the like.

I will complain, yet praise;
I will bewail, approve;
And all my sour-sweet days
I will lament, and love.

George Herbert

A just plea against the just Lord

Thou art indeed just, Lord, if I contend
With thee; but, sir, so what I plead is just.
Why do sinners' ways prosper? and why must
Disappointment all I endeavour end?
    Wert thou my enemy, O thou my friend,
How wouldst thou worse, I wonder, than thou dost
Defeat, thwart me? Oh, the sots and thralls of lust
Do in spare hours more thrive than I that spend,
Sir, life upon thy cause. See, banks and brakes
Now, leavèd how thick! lacèd they are again
With fretty chervil, look, and fresh wind shakes
Them; birds build – but not I build; no, but strain,
Time's eunuch, and not breed one work that wakes.
Mine, O thou lord of life, send my roots rain.

Gerard Manley Hopkins

Discipline

Throw away thy rod,
Throw away thy wrath:
  O my God,
Take the gentle path.

For my heart's desire
Unto thine is bent:
  I aspire
To a full consent.

Though I fail, I weep:
Though I halt in pace,
  Yet I creep
To the throne of grace.

Then let wrath remove;
Love will do the deed:
  For with love
Stony hearts will bleed.

Love is swift of foot;
Love's a man of war,
  And can shoot,
And can hit from far.

Who can 'scape his bow?
That which wrought on thee,
  Brought thee low,
Needs must work on me.

Throw away thy rod;
Though man frailities hath,
  Thou art God:
Throw away thy wrath.

George Herbert

Fain would I say

Fain would I say, 'Forgive my foul offence!'
　　Fain promise never more to disobey;
But, should my Author health again dispense,
　　Again I might desert fair virtue's way;
Again in folly's path might go astray;
　　Again exalt the brute and sink the man;
Then how should I for heavenly mercy pray,
　　Who act so counter heavenly mercy's plan?
Who sin so oft have mourned, yet to temptation ran?

Robert Burns

Forgive the prodigal heart

Behold the prodigal! To thee I come,
To hail my Father and to seek my home.
Nor refuge could I find, nor friend abroad,
Straying in vice and destitute of God.

O let thy terrors and my anguish end!
Be thou my refuge and be thou my friend:
Receive the son thou didst so long reprove,
    Thou that art the God of love!

Matthew Prior

A Hymn to God the Father

Hear me, O God!
    A broken heart
    Is my best part:
Use still thy rod
    That I may prove
    Therein thy love.

If thou hadst not
    Been stern to me,
    But left me free,
I had forgot
    Myself and thee.

For sin's so sweet,
    As minds ill bent
    Rarely repent,
Until they meet
    Their punishment . . .

Sin, Death, and Hell
    His glorious Name
    Quite overcame,
Yet I rebel,
    And slight the same.

But I'll come in,
    Before my loss
    Me farther toss,
As sure to win
    Under his cross.

Ben Jonson

Let us practise your forgiveness, Lord

O holy Jesus who didst for us die,
    And on the altar bleeding lie,
Bearing all torment, pain, reproach and shame,
    That we by virtue of the same,
Though enemies to God, might be
Redeemed, and set at liberty.
    As thou didst us forgive,
So meekly let us love to others show,
    And live in heaven on earth below.

Thomas Traherne

Heaven's sun shining on my soul

But, ah, our sins, our clouds benight the air;
Lord, drain the fens of this my boggy soul,
Whose grosser vapours make my day so foul;
The Son hath strength to chase away
These rising fogs, and make a glorious day:
Rise, and shine always clear; but, most of all
Let me behold thy glory, in thy fall;
That being set, poor I (my flesh being hurled
From this) may meet thee, in another world.

Francis Quarles

Jesus: all that thou didst for love of me

Jesu, sweet is the love of thee,
None other thing so sweet may be;
Nothing that men may hear and see
Hath no sweetness against thee.

Jesu, no song may be sweeter,
Nothing in heartè blissfuller,
Nought may be felt delightfuller,
Than thou, so sweet a lover.

Jesu, thy love was us so free
That it from heaven broughtè thee;
For love thou dear boughtest me,
For love thou hung on rood tree.

Jesu, for love thou tholed'st wrong,
Woundès sore, and painès strong;
Thinè painès were full long –
No man may them tell, nor song.

Jesu, my love thou wert so free,
All that thou didst for love of me.
What shall I for that yieldè thee?
Thou askest nought but love of me.

Jesu, my God, Jesu my king,
Thou askest me none other thing,
But truè love and heart yearning,
And love-tears with sweet mourning.

Jesu, thy love be all my thought,
Of other thing ne reck me nought;
Then have I thy will all wrought,
That havest me full dear bought.

Anonymous

Trinity Sunday

Lord, who hast formed me out of mud,
    And hast redeemed me through thy blood,
    And sanctified me to do good;

Purge all my sins done heretofore:
    For I confess my heavy score,
    And I will strive to sin no more.

Enrich my heart, mouth, hands in me,
    With faith, with hope, with charity;
    That I may run, rise, rest with thee.

George Herbert

A Hymn to God the Father

Wilt thou forgive that sin where I begun,
   Which is my sin, though it were done before?
Wilt thou forgive those sins through which I run,
   And do them still, though still I do deplore?
     When thou hast done, thou hast not done,
      For I have more.

Wilt thou forgive that sin by which I won
   Others to sin, and made my sin their door?
Wilt thou forgive that sin which I did shun
   A year or two, but wallowed in a score?
     When thou hast done, thou hast not done,
      For I have more.

I have a sin of fear, that when I've spun
   My last thread, I shall perish on the shore;
Swear by thyself that at my death thy Sun
   Shall shine as it shines now, and heretofore;
     And having done that, thou hast done,
      I have no more.

John Donne

The Good Shepherd

Christ who knows all his sheep
Will all in safety keep;
He will not lose his blood,
    Nor intercession:
Nor we the purchased good
    Of his dear Passion.

I know my God is just,
To him I wholly trust
All that I have and am,
    All that I hope for.
All's sure and seen to him,
    Which I here grope for.

Lord Jesus, take my spirit:
I trust thy love and merit:
Take home this wandering sheep,
    For thou hast sought it:
This soul in safety keep,
    For thou hast bought it.

Richard Baxter

4. AND IN THE HOUR OF DEATH

But deliver us from evil

The hard gate of dying – And after death?

Be not afraid to pray – to pray is right,
Pray, if thou canst, with hope; but ever pray,
Though hope be weak, or sick with long delay;
Pray in the darkness, if there be no light.

Hartley Coleridge

Be near me on the dark verge of life

Be near me when my light is low,
  When the blood creeps, and the nerves prick
  And tingle; and the heart is sick,
And all the wheels of Being slow.

Be near me when the sensuous frame
  Is racked with pangs that conquer trust;
  And Time, a maniac scattering dust,
And Life, a Fury slinging flame.

Be near me when my faith is dry,
  And men the flies of latter spring,
  That lay their eggs, and sting and sing
And weave their petty cells and die.

Be near me when I fade away,
  To point the term of human strife,
  And on the low dark verge of life
The twilight of eternal day.

Alfred Lord Tennyson

Mercy in our time

Let not mistaken mercy
blind my fading sight,
no false euphoria lull me.
I would not unprepared
take this last journey.
Give me a light to guide me
through dark valleys,
a staff to lean upon,
bread to sustain me,
a blessing in my ear
that fear may not assail me.
Then leaving do not hold my hand,
I go to meet a friend –
    that same who traced
  compassion in the sand.

Nancy Hopkins

Hymn to God my God, in my Sickness

Since I am coming to that Holy room,
    Where, with thy Quire of Saints for evermore,
I shall be made thy Music; As I come
    I tune the Instrument here at the door,
    And what I must do then, think here before.

Whilst my Physicians by their love are grown
    Cosmographers, and I their Map, who lie
Flat on this bed, that by them may be shown
    That this is my South-west discovery
    Per fretum febris, by these straits to die,

I joy, that in these straits, I see my West;
    For, though their currents yield return to none,
What shall my West hurt me? As West and East
    In all flat Maps (and I am one) are one,
    So death doth touch the Resurrection.

Is the Pacific Sea my home? Or are
    The Eastern riches? Is Jerusalem?
Anyan, and Magellan, and Gibraltar,
    All straits, and none but straits, are ways to them,
    Whether where Japhet dwelt, or Cham, or Sem.

We think that Paradise and Calvary,
    Christ's Cross, and Adam's tree, stood in one
        place;
Look, Lord, and find both Adams met in me;
    As the first Adam's sweat surrounds my face,
    May the Last Adam's blood my soul embrace.

So, in his purple wrapped receive me Lord,
    By these his thorns give me his other Crown;
And as to others' souls I preached thy word,
    Be this my Text, my Sermon to mine own,
    Therefore that he may raise the Lord throws down.

John Donne

The Angel of the Agony speaks

Jesu! by that shuddering dread which fell on thee;
Jesu! by that cold dismay which sicken'd thee;
Jesu! by that pang of heart which thrill'd in thee;
Jesu! by that mount of sins which crippled thee;
Jesu! by that sense of guilt which stifled thee;
Jesu! by that innocence which girdled thee;
Jesu! by that sanctity which reign'd in thee;
Jesu! by that Godhead which was one with thee;
Jesu! spare these souls which are so dear to thee,
Who in prison, calm and patient, wait for thee;
Hasten, Lord, their hour, and bid them come to thee,
To that glorious home, where they shall ever gaze on
    thee.

John Henry Newman

Pray for us now and at the hour of our death

Because I do not hope to turn again
Let these words answer
For what is done, not to be done again
May the judgement not be too heavy upon us

Because these wings are no longer wings to fly
But merely vans to beat the air
The air which is now thoroughly small and dry
Smaller and dryer than the will
Teach us to care and not to care
Teach us to sit still.

Pray for us sinners now and at the hour of our death
Pray for us now and at the hour of our death.

T. S. Eliot

A Prayer before Death

I give you thanks, Lord God of nations,
For all the worldly joys which I have known.
But now, gracious Maker, I have the greatest need
That you grant my spirit to God,
That my soul may set out to you,
Prince of Angels, going in peace
Into your power. I pray
That the hell-fiends may not humiliate me.

Anonymous (from The Battle of Maldon,
written soon after 991)

Bereavement

They are all gone into the world of light!
    And I alone sit lingering here;
Their very memory is fair and bright,
    And my sad thoughts doth clear.

It glows and glitters in my cloudy breast
    Like stars upon some gloomy grove,
Or those faint beams in which this hill is dressed,
    After the sun's remove.

I see them walking in an air of glory,
    Whose light doth trample on my days:
My days, which are at best but dull and hoary,
    Mere glimmering and decays.

O holy Hope! and high Humility,
    High as the heavens above!
These are your walks, and you have showed them
me,
    To kindle my cold love.

Dear beauteous Death! the jewel of the Just,
    Shining nowhere but in the dark;
What mysteries do lie beyond thy dust,
    Could man outlook that mark! . . .

O Father of eternal life, and all
    Created glories under thee!
Resume thy spirit from this world of thrall
    Into true liberty.

Either disperse these mists, which blot and fill
    My perspective still as they pass,
Or else remove me hence unto that hill,
    Where I shall need no glass.

Henry Vaughan

Come quickly, Lord, and take me

Never weather-beaten sail more willing bent to shore,
  Never tired pilgrim's limbs affected slumber more,
Than my weary sprite now longs to fly out of my
      troubled breast,
O come quickly, sweetest Lord, and take my soul to
      rest!

Ever blooming are the joys of heaven's high paradise,
Cold age deafs not there our ears nor vapour dims
      our eyes:
Glory there the sun outshines; whose beams the
      blessèd only see,
O come quickly, glorious Lord, and raise my sprite to
      thee!

Thomas Campion

'Strong Son of God'

Strong Son of God, immortal Love,
    Whom we, that have not seen thy face,
    By faith, and faith alone, embrace,
Believing where we cannot prove; . . .

Thou wilt not leave us in the dust:
    Thou madest man, he knows not why,
    He thinks he was not made to die;
And thou hast made him: thou are just.

Thou seemest human and divine,
    The highest, holiest manhood, thou:
    Our wills are ours, we know not how;
Our wills are ours, to make them thine.

Our little systems have their day;
    They have their day and cease to be;
    They are but broken lights of thee,
And thou, O Lord, art more than they.

We have but faith: we cannot know;
    For knowledge is of things we see;
    And yet we trust it comes from thee,
A beam in darkness: let it grow.

Let knowledge grow from more to more,
    But more of reverence in us dwell;
    That mind and soul, according well,
May make one music as before,

But vaster. We are fools and slight;
    We mock thee when we do not fear:
    But help thy foolish ones to bear;
Help thy vain worlds to bear thy light.

Alfred Lord Tennyson

At the last trumpet

At the round earth's imagined corners, blow
Your trumpets, Angels, and arise, arise
From death, you numberless infinities
Of souls, and to your scattered bodies go,
All whom the flood did, and fire shall o'erthrow,
All whom war, dearth, age, agues, tyrannies,
Despair, law, chance, hath slain, and you whose eyes
Shall behold God, and never taste death's woe.
But let them sleep, Lord, and me mourn a space,
For, if above all these, my sins abound,
'Tis late to ask abundance of thy grace,
When we are there; here on this lowly ground,
Teach me how to repent; for that's as good
As if thou'hadst sealed my pardon, with thy blood.

John Donne

Dies Irae

That day of wrath, that dreadful day,
When heaven and earth shall pass away,
What power shall be the sinner's stay?
How shall he meet that dreadful day?

When, shrivelling like a parchèd scroll,
The flaming heavens together roll;
When louder yet, and yet more dread,
Swells the high trump that wakes the dead;

Oh! on that day, that wrathful day,
When man to judgement wakes from clay,
Be THOU the trembling sinner's stay,
Though heaven and earth shall pass away!

Sir Walter Scott

Peace

My soul, there is a country
   Far beyond the stars,
Where stands a wingèd sentry
   All skilful in the wars:
There, above noise and danger,
   Sweet Peace sits crowned with smiles,
And One born in a manger
   Commands the beauteous files.
He is thy gracious Friend,
   And – O my soul, awake –
Did in pure love descend
   To die here for thy sake.
If thou canst get but thither,
   There grows the flower of Peace,
The Rose that cannot wither,
   Thy fortress, and thy ease.
Leave then thy foolish ranges;
   For none can thee secure
But One who never changes –
   Thy God, thy life, thy cure.

Henry Vaughan

Old Shepherd's Prayer

Up to the bed by the window, where I be lyin',
Comes bells and bleat of the flock wi' they two
   children's claek.
Over, from under the eaves there's the starlings
   flyin',
And down in yard, fit to burst his chain, yapping out
   at Sue I do hear young Mac.

Turning around like a falled-over sack
I can see team ploughin' in Whithy-bush field and
   meal carts startin' up road to Church-Town;
Saturday arternoon the men goin' back
And the women from market, trapin' home over the
   down.

Heavenly Master, I wud like to wake to they same
   green places
Where I be know'd for breakin' dogs and follerin'
   sheep.
And if I may not walk in th' old ways and look on th'
   old faces
I wud sooner sleep.

Charlotte Mew

Last Lines

The last lines my sister Emily ever wrote (note by Charlotte Brontë).

No coward soul is mine,
No trembler in the world's storm-troubled sphere:
I see Heaven's glories shine,
And faith shines equal, arming me from fear.

O God within my breast,
Almighty, ever-present Deity!
Life – that in me has rest,
As I – undying Life – have power in Thee!

Vain are the thousand creeds
That move men's hearts: unutterably vain;
Worthless as withered weeds,
Or idlest froth amid the boundless main,

To waken doubt in one
Holding so fast by Thine infinity;
So surely anchored on
The steadfast rock of immortality.

With wide-embracing love
Thy spirit animates eternal years,
Pervades and broods above,
Changes, sustains, dissolves, creates, and rears.

Though earth and man were gone,
And suns and universes ceased to be,
And Thou were left alone,
Every existence would exist in Thee.

There is not room for Death,
Nor atom that his might could render void:
Thou–THOU art Being and Breath,
And what THOU art may never be destroyed.

Emily Brontë

The Passionate Man's Pilgrimage

*Supposed to be Written by One at the
Point of Death*

Give me my Scallop shell of quiet,
My staff of Faith to walk upon,
My Scrip of Joy, Immortal diet,
My bottle of salvation:
My Gown of Glory, hope's true gage,
And thus I'll take my pilgrimage . . .

From thence to heaven's Bribeless hall
Where no corrupted voices brawl,
No Conscience molten into gold,
Nor forged accusers bought and sold,
No cause deferred, nor vain spent journey,
For there Christ is the King's Attorney:
Who pleads for all without degrees,
And he hath Angels, but no fees.

When the grand twelve million Jury,
Of our sins with dreadful fury,
'Gainst our souls black verdicts give,
Christ pleads his death, and then we live,
Be thou my speaker, taintless pleader,
Unblotted Lawyer, true proceeder,
Thou movest salvation even for alms:
Not with a bribed Lawyer's palms.

And this is my eternal plea,
To him that made Heaven, Earth and Sea,
Seeing my flesh must die so soon,
And want a head to dine next noon,
Just at the stroke when my veins start and spread
Set on my soul an everlasting head.
Then am I ready like a palmer fit,
To tread those blest paths which before I writ.

Sir Walter Raleigh

A Prayer

Grant, I thee pray, such heat into mine heart
That to this love of thine may be equàl;
Grant me from Satan's service to astart,
With whom me rueth so long to have been thrall;
Grant me, good Lord and Creator of all,
The flame to quench of all sinful desire
And in thy love set all mine heart afire.

That when the journey of this deadly life
My silly ghost hath finishèd, and thence
Departen must without his fleshly wife,
Alone into his Lordès high presènce,
He may thee find, O well of indulgènce,
In thy lordship not as a lord, but rather
As a very tender, loving father.

Sir Thomas More

5. CELEBRATIONS AND MYSTERIES

For yours is the kingdom, the power and the glory

Prayers at Christmas – Prayers at Easter

The off'rings of the Eastern kings of old
Unto our Lord were incense, myrrh and gold;
Incense because a God; gold as a king;
And myrrh as to a dying man they bring.
Instead of incense (Blessed Lord) if we
Can send a sigh or fervent prayer to thee,
Instead of myrrh if we can but provide
Tears that from penitential eyes do slide,
And though we have no gold, if for our part
We can present thee with a broken heart
Thou wilt accept: and say those Eastern kings
Did not present thee with more precious things.

Nathaniel Wanley

Northumbrian Sequence IV

Let in the wind
Let in the rain
Let in the moors tonight,

The storm beats on my window-pane,
Night stands at my bed-foot,
Let in the fear,

Let in the pain,
Let in the trees that toss and groan,
Let in the north tonight.

Let in the nameless formless power
That beats upon my door,
Let in the ice, let in the snow,
The banshee howling on the moor,
The bracken-bush on the bleak hillside,
Let in the dead tonight

The whistling ghost behind the dyke,
The dead that rot in mire,
Let in the thronging ancestors
The unfulfilled desire,
Let in the wraith of the dead earl,
Let in the dead tonight.

Let in the cold,
Let in the wet,
Let in the loneliness,
Let in the quick,
Let in the dead,
Let in the unpeopled skies.

Oh how can virgin fingers weave
A covering for the void,
How can my fearful heart conceive
Gigantic solitude?
How can a house so small contain
A company so great?
Let in the dark,
Let in the dead,
Let in your love tonight.

Let in the snow that numbs the grave,
Let in the acorn-tree,
The mountain stream and mountain stone,
Let in the bitter sea.

Fearful is my virgin heart
And frail my virgin form,
And must I then take pity on
The raging of the storm
That rose up from the great abyss
Before the earth was made,
That pours the stars in cataracts
And shakes this violent world?

Let in the fire,
Let in the power,
Let in the invading might.

Gentle must my fingers be
And pitiful my heart
Since I must bind in human form
A living power so great,
A living impulse great and wild
That cries about my house
With all the violence of desire
Desiring this my peace.

Pitiful my heart must hold
The lonely stars at rest,
Have pity on the raven's cry
The torrent and the eagle's wing,
The icy water of the tarn
And on the biting blast.

Let in the wound,
Let in the pain,
Let in your child tonight.

Kathleen Raine

Hymn for Advent

Lord, come away!
    Why dost thou stay?
Thy road is ready; and thy paths made straight
    With longing expectations wait
The consecration of thy beauteous feet.
    Ride on triumphantly; behold, we lay
    Our lusts and proud will in thy way!

Hosanna! Welcome to our hearts! Lord, here
Thou hast a temple too; and full as dear
As that of Sion, and as full of sin:
Nothing but thieves and robbers dwell therein:
Enter, and chase them forth, and cleanse the floor:
Crucify them, that they may never more
        Profane That holy place
    Where thou hast chose to set thy face!
    And then if our stiff tongues shall be
        Mute in the praises of thy Deity,
        The stones out of the Temple wall
            Shall cry aloud and call
    Hosanna! And thy glorious footsteps greet!

Jeremy Taylor

Christmas gift

Moonless darkness stands between.
Past, O Past, no more be seen!
But the Bethlehem star may lead me
To the sight of him who freed me
From the self that I have been.
Make me pure, Lord: thou art holy;
Make me meek, Lord: thou wert lowly;
Now beginning, and alway;
Now begin, on Christmas day.

Gerard Manley Hopkins

At Bethlehem

Come, we shepherds, whose blest sight
   Hath met Love's noon in nature's night;
Come, lift we up our loftier song,
And wake the sun that lies too long.

Gloomy night embraced the place
   Where the noble Infant lay:
The Babe looked up and showed his face;
   In spite of darkness, it was day: –
It was thy Day, Sweet! and did rise
Not from the east, but from thine eyes.

We saw thee in thy balmy nest,
   Young dawn of our eternal day;
We saw thine eyes break from their east,
   And chase the trembling shades away;
   We saw thee, (and we bless the sight),
We saw thee by thine own sweet light.

Welcome, all wonders in one sight!
   Eternity shut in a span!
Summer in winter! Day in night!
Heaven in earth! and God in man!
Great Little One, whose all-embracing birth,
Lifts earth to heaven, stoops heaven to earth.

Richard Crashaw

The Nativity of Our Lord and Saviour Jesus Christ

Where is this stupendous stranger?
  Swains of Solyma, advise,
Lead me to my Master's manger,
  Shew me where my Saviour lies.

O most Mighty! O most Holy!
  Far beyond the seraph's thought,
Art thou then so mean and lowly,
  As unheeded prophets taught?

O the magnitude of meekness!
  Worth from worth immortal sprung;
O the strength of infant weakness,
  If eternal is so young! . . .

Nature's decorations glisten
  Far above their usual trim;
Birds on box and laurels listen,
  As so near the cherubs hymn . . .

Spinks and ouzels sing sublimely
  'We too have a Saviour born';
Whiter blossoms burst untimely
  On the blest Mosaic thorn.

God all-bounteous, all creative,
  Whom no ills from good dissuade,
Is incarnate and a native
  Of the very world he made.

Christopher Smart

Victory

Down to that littleness, down to all that
Crying and hunger, all that tiny flesh
And flickering spirit – down the great stars fall,
Here the huge kings bow.
Here the farmer sees his fragile lambs,
Here the wise man throws his books away.

This manger is the universe's cradle,
This singing mother has the words of truth.
Here the ox and ass and sparrow stop,
Here the hopeless man breaks into trust.
God, you have made a victory for the lost.
Give us this daily Bread, this little Host.

Elizabeth Jennings

Thou who createdst everything

Thou who createdst everything,
Sweet Father, heavenly King,
Hear me – I, thy son, implore:
For Man this flesh and bone I bore.

Clear and bright my breast and side,
Blood over whiteness spilling wide,
Holes in my body crucified.

Stiff and stark my long arms rise,
Dimness and darkness cloud my eyes;
Like sculpted marble hang my thighs.

Red my feet with the flowing blood,
Holes in them washed through with that flood.
Mercy on Man's sins, Father on high!
Through all my wounds to thee I cry!

Anonymous, 13th century, translated by Donald Davie

Sonnet

I am not moved to love thee, my Lord God,
by the Heaven thou hast promised me:
I am not moved by the sore dreaded hell
to forbear me from offending thee.

I am moved by thee, Lord; I am moved
at seeing thee nailed upon the cross and mocked:
I am moved by thy body all over wounds:
I am moved by thy dishonour and thy death.

I am moved, last, by thy love, in such a wise
that though there were no heaven I still should love
    thee,
and though there were no hell I still should fear thee.

I need no gift of thee to make me love thee;
For though my present hope were all despair,
As now I love thee I should love thee still.

Miguel de Guavera, translated by Samuel Beckett

O Deus Ego Amo Te

O God, I love thee, I love thee –
Not out of hope of heaven for me
Nor fearing not to love and be
   In the everlasting burning.
Thou, thou, my Jesus, after me
   Didst reach thine arms out dying,
For my sake sufferedst nails and lance,
Mocked and marrèd countenance,
   Sorrows passing number,
   Sweat and care and cumber,
Yea and death, and this for me,
   And thou couldst see me sinning:
Then I, why should not I love thee,
Jesu, so much in love with me?
Not for heaven's sake; not to be
Out of hell by loving thee;
Not for any gains I see;
But just the way that thou didst me
I do love and I will love thee;
What must I love thee, Lord, for then?
For being my king and God. Amen.

Gerard Manley Hopkins

Easter Jesus, make me love thee

Jesu Lord, that madest me,
    And with thy blessèd blood me bought,
Forgive that I have grievèd thee
    With word, will, work or thought.

Jesu, for thy woundès' smart
    On foot and on hands two,
Make me meek and low in heart,
    And thee to love as I should do . . .

Jesu, for thy doleful tears,
    That thou weptest for my guilt,
Hear and speed my prayers
    And spare me that I be not spilt.

Jesu, for them I thee beseech
    That wrathen thee in any wise;
Withhold from them thine hand of wreche
    And let them end in thy service.

Jesu, joyful for to seen,
    With thy saints every one,
Comfort all that careful been,
    And help them that been woebegone.

Jesu, keep them that been good,
    And mend them that have grievèd thee,
And send them fruits and earthly food,
    As each man needeth in his degree.

Jesu, that art withouten lees
    Almighty God in Trinity,
Cease these wars and send us peace,
With lasting love and charity . . .

Jesu, for thy blessèd blood,
    Bring those souls into bliss
For whom I have had any good,
    And spare them that they have done amiss.

Anonymous, about 1400

The Lord's Prayer

'Give us this day.' Give us this day and night.
Give us the bread, the sky. Give us the power
To bend and not be broken by your light.

And let us soothe and sway like the new flower
Which closes, opens to the night, the day,
Which stretches up and rides upon a power

More than its own, whose freedom is the play
Of light, for whom the earth and air are bread.
Give us the shorter night, the longer day.

In thirty years so many words were spread,
And miracles. An undefeated death
Has passed as Easter passed, but those words said

Finger our doubt and run along our breath.

Elizabeth Jennings

On the Cross

Thy restless feet now cannot go
  For us and our eternal good,
As they were ever wont. What though
  They swim, alas! in their own flood!

Thy hands to give thou canst not lift,
  Yet will thy hand still giving be;
It gives, but O, itself's the gift!
  It gives though bound, though bound 'tis free!

Richard Crashaw

Good Friday 1613. Riding Westward

Let man's Soul be a Sphere, and then, in this,
The intelligence that moves, devotion is,
And as the other Spheres, by being grown
Subject to foreign motions, lose their own,
And being by others hurried every day,
Scarce in a year their natural form obey:
Pleasure or business, so, our Souls admit
For their first mover, and are whirled by it.
Hence is 't, that I am carried towards the West
This day, when my Soul's form bends toward the
    East.
There I should see a Sun, by rising set,
And by that setting endless day beget;
But that Christ on this Cross, did rise and fall,
Sin had eternally benighted all . . .

O Saviour, as Thou hang'st upon the tree;
I turn my back to Thee, but to receive
Corrections, till Thy mercies bid Thee leave.
O think me worth Thine anger, punish me,
Burn off my rusts, and my deformity,
Restore Thine Image, so much, by Thy grace,
That Thou may'st know me, and I'll turn my face.

John Donne

Easter

Most glorious Lord of life, that on this day
  Didst make thy triumph over death and sin;
  And having harrowed hell didst bring away
  Captivity thence captive, us to win:
This joyous day, dear Lord, with joy begin,
  And grant that we for whom thou diddest die
  Being with thy dear blood clean washed from sin,
  May live forever in felicity.
  And that thy love we weighing worthily,
    May likewise love thee for the same again;
    And for thy sake that all like dear didst buy,
    With love may one another entertain.
So let us love, dear love, like as we ought.
Love is the lesson which the Lord us taught.

Edmund Spenser

6. EPILOGUE: GLIMPSES AND LONGINGS

For ever and ever. Amen.

I would have no stained glass saints in my cathedral
Preferring that there be children of light, always
Active, listening and attentive; I would have no books
Of prayers, torn and shredded at the edges, no old songs,
No plate, chipped pews, bookstall or notice-board,
No thundering status of organ, orators, candles or wands:

But my west window would be the light-patched coat of
*   cloud*
Bringing calm after a day's rain; yellow chasing grey,
*   weather clearing to*
High light-blue, aerial as a lark, slabbed with reds,
*   sunset-water*
And a sound like wind, rippling, running and sighing-over
Beach and channel and shallow sand, lifting the birds,
*   moulding*
Sand-rib and dune, pouring out a tide, whistling, changing
As we shall rise, meeting the Lord in the air, becoming
Light as birds, numberless, parents of time, endless.

Martyn Halsall

To God the Whole Reality

O Living Love replacing phantasy,
O Joy of life revealed in Love's creation;
Our mood of longing turns to indication:
Space is the Whom our loves are needed by,
Time is our choice of How to love and Why.

W. H. Auden

Clarify

Clarify me, please,
God of the galaxies,
Make me a meteor,
Or else a metaphor

So lively that it grows
Beyond its likeness and
Stands on its own, a land
That nobody can lose.

God, give me liberty
But not so much that I
See you on Calvary,
Nailed to the wood by me.

Elizabeth Jennings

The Prayer of Daft Harry

Lord, since this world is filled with fire,
    Inside this rounded mould –
Let's turn it inside out, O Lord,
    While hands and feet are cold.

Let's split the world in half, O Lord,
    As open as my palm,
Until the snow has melted down,
    And hands and feet are warm.

Let's turn the world all inside out,
    And glorify Our Name;
Until Our fire makes Jesus laugh,
    While I blow up the flame.

Let's do it now, this minute, Lord,
    And make a glorious blaze:
Till Jesus laughs and claps his hands,
    While Mary sings Our praise!

W. H. Davies

Twice

I took my heart in my hand
    (O my love, O my love),
I said: Let me fall or stand,
    Let me live or die,
But this once hear me speak –
    (O my love, O my love) –
Yet a woman's words are weak;
    You should speak, not I.

You took my heart in your hand
    With a friendly smile,
With a critical eye you scann'd,
    Then set it down.
And said: 'It is still unripe,
    Better wait awhile;
Wait while the skylarks pipe,
    Till the corn grows brown.'

As you set it down it broke –
    Broke, but I did not wince;
I smiled at the speech you spoke,
    At your judgement that I heard:
But I have not often smiled
    Since then, nor question'd since,
Nor cared for cornflowers wild,
    Nor sung with the singing bird.

I take my heart in my hand,
    O my God, O my God,
My broken heart in my hand:
    Thou hast seen, judge thou.
My hope was written on sand,
    O my God, O my God:
Now let thy judgement stand –
    Yea, judge me now.

I take my heart in my hand –
  I shall not die, but live –
Before thy face I stand;
  I, for thou callest such:
All that I have I bring,
  All that I am I give,
Smile thou and I shall sing,
  But shall not question much.

Christina Rossetti

Walking with God

Oh! for a closer walk with God,
  A calm and heavenly frame;
A light to shine upon the road
  That leads me to the Lamb!

Where is the blessedness I knew
  When first I saw the Lord?
Where is the soul-refreshing view
  Of Jesus and his word?

What peaceful hours I once enjoyed!
  How sweet their memory still!
But they have left an aching void,
  The world can never fill.

Return, O holy Dove, return,
  Sweet messenger of rest;
I hate the sins that made thee mourn,
  And drove thee from my breast.

The dearest idol I have known,
  Whate'er that idol be;
Help me to tear it from thy throne,
  And worship only thee.

So shall my walk be close with God,
  Calm and serene my frame;
So purer light shall mark the road
  That leads me to the Lamb.

William Cowper

A Journey Spell

I guard myself with this rod and give myself into
    God's protection,
Against the painful stroke, against the grievous
    stroke,
Against the grim dread,
Against the great terror which is hateful to each,
And against all evil which may enter the land.
I chant a charm of victory, I bear a rod of victory,
Word-victory, work-victory. May they be of power for
    me . . .
I pray now to the God of victory, to the mercy of God,
For a good journey, a mild and gentle
Wind from these shores. I have heard of winds
Which rouse whirling waters. Thus ever preserved
From all fiends may I meet friends,
So that I may dwell in the Almighty's protection,
Guarded from the enemy who seeks my life,
Set amid the glory of the angels,
And in the holy hand of the Mighty One of heaven,
Whilst I may live in this life. Amen.

*Anonymous; from a selection of Charms
in the Anglo Saxon* Exeter Book

These verses following were completed by Sir Walter Raleigh the night before he died and left at the Gate house

Even such is time which takes in trust
Our youth, our joys, and all we have,
And pays us but with age and dust:
Who in the dark and silent grave
When we have wandered all our ways
Shuts up the story of our days.
And from which earth and grave and dust
The Lord shall raise me up I trust.

Sir Walter Raleigh

Hymnus

God be in my head
   And in my understanding,
God be in mine eyes
   And in my looking,
God be in my mouth
   And in my speaking,
God be in my heart
   And in my thinking,
God be at mine end
   And at my departing.

Anonymous

ACKNOWLEDGEMENTS

Every effort has been made to trace the copyright holders of material quoted in this book. Information on any omissions should be sent to the publishers who will make full acknowledgement in future editions.

The compiler and publishers are pleased to acknowledge the following for permission to quote from their copyright material:

Faber and Faber Ltd for W. H. Auden, extract from *For the Time Being: A Christmas Oratorio*; and for T. S. Eliot, extract from *Ash Wednesday* from *Collected Poems 1909–1962* (1963).

Indiana University Press for Samuel Beckett's translation of Myguel de Guavera from *Anthology of Mexican Poetry* published by Thames and Hudson, (1959).

Carcanet Press Ltd for Donald Davie 'If I take the Wings of the Morning' from *To Scorch or Freeze* (1988).

Donald Davie for two translations from *The New Oxford Book of Christian Verse*. © Donald Davie 1981.

The Society of Authors and the literary trustees of Walter de la Mare for 'Dust' from *Collected Poems*. The Society of Authors on behalf of the copyright owner, Mrs Iris Wise, for 'Student Taper' by James Stephens.

Victor Gollancz Ltd for the translation of Cynewulf from *God of a Hundred Names* edited by Barbara Greene and Victor Gollancz (1962).

David Higham Associates for Elizabeth Jennings 'Clarify', 'Victory', 'The Lord's Prayer' and 'Prayer yet could be a dance'; for John Masefield, extract from 'The Everlasting Mercy'.

Collins Publishers Ltd for 'O thou that art unwearying' and 'He whom I bow to' by C. S. Lewis.

SCM Press Ltd for 'Christ the Cornerstone' from *A Treasury of Christian Verse* edited by Hugh Martin (1959).

Curtis Brown Ltd for Grace Nichols 'Caribbean Woman Prayer'.

126

Ruth Pitter for 'Help, Good Shepherd' from *Urania* published by Cresett Press Ltd (1951).

Hamish Hamilton Ltd for 'Northumbrian Sequence IV' from *The Collected Poems of Kathleen Raine* (1956).

Edith Forrest for 'Thanksgiving', Martyn Halsall for 'Ex-Cathedra', Nancy Hopkins for 'Mercy in our Time' and M. J. Norman for 'Prayer'.

INDEX OF POETS

INDEX OF FIRST LINES